AF486360

GRIT

GRIT

DERRICK C SOLANO

CONTENTS

Dedication   X

Acknowledgments   xi

Preface: Why GRIT Matters   xiii

PART ONE: SCARS   1

The Truth About Scars   3

Wear Them Like Armor   7

What They Tried to Break   11

Scars as Stories   15

Prompt   19

PART TWO: FEAR   23

The Lies Fear Tells You   27

Do It Scared   31

Reclaiming Control 35

The Freedom in Letting Go 41

Prompt 45

PART THREE: FIRE 49

The Ashes Don't Define You 51

Fanning the Flames 55

Burn the Bullsh*t 59

The Power of Anger 63

Prompt 67

PART FOUR: RESILIENCE 71

What Resilience Really Is 75

Layering Strength 79

The Unseen Work 83

Living Unbreakably 87

Prompt 93

PART FIVE: FREEDOM 97

Owning Your Truth 101

Rewriting Your Narrative 105

Loving Yourself Loudly	109

The Joy of Imperfection	115

Prompt	121

Final Affirmation	125
Acknowledgments	127
About the Author	128

To the warriors who battle in silence,
the ones who carry scars the world tried to
shame,
and the souls who refuse to stay down—
this is for you.

**You are proof that strength isn't about
perfection; it's about rising, fighting, and
thriving, no matter what.**

Acknowledgments

To Anthony, my rock, my partner, and my unwavering source of love—thank you for standing beside me through every storm and for reminding me what true strength and loyalty look like. To my family, both chosen and unexpected, your support has carried me further than words could ever express.

To the readers who pick up this book and dare to embrace their imperfections, this is for you. Your courage to face life's hardest battles and your refusal to stay down inspire everything I write. Thank you for letting my story be part of yours. Together, we prove that resilience is not just possible—it's unstoppable.

And to my past self—the scared, lost, and angry kid who thought he'd never be enough—you made it. Every scar, every heartbreak, every fall built this strength. I'll never stop thanking you for surviving.

Preface: Why GRIT Matters

Life doesn't wait for you to be ready. It hits, and it hits hard. I know because I've been there—at rock bottom, stripped of everything I thought made me who I was. I've faced the kind of pain that leaves scars, the kind that makes you question if you'll ever stand again. But here's the thing about scars: they don't just mark you; they make you. They're proof that you've been through hell—and survived.

This book exists because of those scars—mine and yours. It's not about perfection or pretending everything's okay. It's about getting real with yourself, embracing the mess, and finding strength in the chaos. I wrote *GRIT* to remind you that resilience isn't some lofty ideal; it's something you build every single day, piece by piece, layer by layer.

This isn't a self-help book that sugarcoats life's challenges or promises quick fixes. It's a pocket-sized manifesto for those moments when the world feels like it's falling apart, and you need something—anything—to hold on to. Whether you're battling fear, breaking free from the weight of perfectionism, or just trying to make it through one more day, this book is here to remind you: you're not alone, and you're stronger than you think.

GRIT is the product of a life lived in the fire and rebuilt from the ashes. It's for anyone who's ever been told they're too broken, too damaged, or too lost to be found. It's proof that even when life knocks you down, you can rise again—stronger, fiercer, and unbreakable. This is your guide to owning your scars, confronting your fears, and turning every ounce of pain into the fuel that keeps you moving forward. Let's get to work.

PART ONE: SCARS

"Your scars don't make you weak. They prove you survived."

Scars tell a story—your story. They're not just marks on your skin or memories in your mind; they're evidence of the battles you've fought and the strength you've earned. Society might try to shame them, hide them, or erase them, but in truth, your scars are your armor. They're not there to remind you of pain—they're there to remind you of resilience.

This section is about stepping out of the shadows of your past and into the light of your strength. It's about owning every part of your journey, even the messy, painful, and broken parts, and recognizing that they've shaped the fighter you are today. You don't have to hide your scars. You wear them like a crown, a testament to the life you've lived and the battles you've survived.

Your past doesn't define you, but how you rise from it does. Let's take those scars and turn them into symbols of power.

The Truth About Scars

Why hiding your pain only makes it harder to heal

Scars—physical or emotional—aren't flaws; they're proof of survival. Yet, so many of us go to great lengths to hide them. We cover them up, bury the memories behind them, and pretend they don't exist. But here's the hard truth: hiding your scars doesn't erase the pain that caused them. It traps it, leaving it to fester and weigh you down.

Healing starts with acknowledgment. By hiding your pain, you're denying yourself the chance to process it, learn from it, and ultimately grow stronger because of it. Scars are not signs of weakness; they're signs of resilience. They show where you've been hurt, yes, but more importantly, they show that you've healed enough to keep going.

Think about it: a wound that's ignored doesn't just disappear—it worsens. But when you face it, clean it, and give it time to heal, it becomes part of you, stronger than before. The same goes for the emotional scars we carry. Hiding them might feel like protection, but it's really a barrier to freedom. You're not protecting yourself—you're holding yourself back.

Owning your scars means facing the pain that caused them and choosing to see the strength they represent. Each scar is a chapter in your story, a reminder that you made it through something that tried to break you. It's not about glorifying the pain—it's about honoring the healing. Let your scars breathe, let them be seen, and let them remind you of just how far you've come.

Because the truth is, your scars aren't the end of the story—they're proof you've still got more to write.

Wear Them Like Armor

How to reframe scars as a testament to resilience

Scars aren't just reminders of where you've been hurt—they're evidence of what you've overcome. They're not there to shame you; they're there to strengthen you. Each scar, whether physical or emotional, tells a story about a battle you fought—and won. The key is shifting how you see them: from something to hide into something to honor.

When you start to see your scars as symbols of resilience, they transform. They stop being painful reminders of the past and become badges of strength. Think of your scars as your personal armor, forged through the fire of life's hardest moments. They are your proof that no matter how many times you've been knocked down, you got back up. That's power, and it's yours.

This isn't about pretending scars don't hurt or glorifying the pain that caused them. It's about recognizing the strength it took to survive and the healing it took to keep going. Your scars are not signs of weakness—they're marks of growth. Every scar means you lived through something that could've broken you, but it didn't. You're still here.

So, wear them boldly. Let them remind you of your resilience every time you see them. Let them inspire you to face whatever comes next with the same strength. Because when you wear your scars like armor, nothing can touch you. They're not your shame—they're your triumph.

And every time you own them, you prove to yourself and the world: you are unbreakable.

What They Tried to Break

A reflection on times you thought you'd **fall apart but didn't**

Think back to the moments when it felt like the world was against you. The times when everything you relied on was stripped away, and you were left wondering how you'd ever stand again. Maybe it was a betrayal that cut deep, a loss that left you hollow, or a failure so devastating it felt like you'd never recover. In those moments, you might've believed you were broken beyond repair. But here's the truth—you weren't.

The fact that you're reading this right now proves that every time life tried to break you, it failed. Even when you thought you couldn't keep going, you did. Even when it felt like you had nothing left, you found a way to rebuild. Maybe it wasn't pretty, maybe it wasn't graceful, but you did it. And that's where your strength lies—not in avoiding the fall, but in getting back up every single time.

What they—whether "they" is a person, a system, or even your own self-doubt—tried to break was the part of you that keeps fighting, that keeps believing, that refuses to quit. And no matter how many hits you've taken, that part of you is still here. Bruised, maybe. Scarred, definitely. But still standing.

So reflect on those moments. Not to relive the pain, but to recognize the power you showed in surviving them. Think of all the times you thought you were done, only to prove yourself wrong. Those moments don't define you, but they built you. And every step forward, no matter how small, was a victory they couldn't take from you.

Because no matter what life threw at you, you didn't fall apart—you rose.

14 – DERRICK C SOLANO

Scars as Stories

How sharing your story can heal both you and others

Every scar you carry tells a story—a story of pain, survival, and resilience. It's easy to think that keeping those stories hidden is a form of protection, but the truth is, sharing them can be one of the most healing acts for both yourself and the people around you.

When you share your story, you take control of it. You reclaim the narrative that pain tried to write for you, and you turn it into something powerful. Speaking about your scars doesn't mean glorifying the pain that caused them; it means honoring the strength it took to survive. It's an act of defiance against shame and a declaration that your scars don't define you—they empower you.

But it's not just about you. Sharing your story creates connection. There's someone out there right now, carrying a similar wound, thinking they're alone in their struggle. Your story could be the thing that makes them realize they're not. It could be the spark that gives them hope, the strength to keep going, and the courage to believe in their own healing.

When we share our scars, we create a ripple effect. We show others that it's okay to be vulnerable, to embrace imperfection, and to find strength in the messiness of life. And as we help others heal, we often find that we're healing ourselves in the process. Speaking your truth doesn't erase the pain, but it transforms it—it turns it into something useful, something meaningful, something real.

Your scars are stories of survival, resilience, and transformation. By sharing them, you remind yourself—and others—that healing is possible and strength is contagious.

Because every time you tell your story, you light the way for someone else to find their own.

18 – DERRICK C SOLANO

Prompt

Take a moment to reflect on one scar you carry—whether it's physical or emotional. Think about where it came from, what it represents, and how it has shaped the person you are today.

Now, write about it.

- **Describe the scar:** What does it look like? How does it feel when you see it or think about it?
- **Revisit the story behind it:** What happened? How did it leave its mark on you?

- **Explore its impact:** How did it change you? What did you learn? What strength did it give you?

Be honest. This is your space to own your story, to confront the pain, and to find the power in what you've endured. There's no right or wrong answer—just you, your scar, and the resilience it represents.

Because every scar carries a lesson, and every lesson adds to your strength.

PART TWO: FEAR

"*Fear is just another kind of fuel.*"

Fear is inevitable. It creeps in when we're at our most vulnerable, whispering doubts, magnifying risks, and convincing us to stay stuck where it's "safe." But here's the truth: fear isn't the enemy—it's a signal. It's a reminder that something matters deeply to you, that you're standing at the edge of growth.

This section is about reframing your relationship with fear. Instead of letting it paralyze you, you'll learn how to let it propel you. Fear doesn't have to hold you back; it can push you forward. It can light a fire under you to move, to act, to prove it wrong.

Courage isn't the absence of fear—it's acting in spite of it. And every time you face it head-on, you take away its power. You become stronger, bolder, and more resilient. Fear will always be there, but so will your ability to rise above it.

Let's stop running from fear and start using it as fuel to drive us toward the life we're meant to live.

The Lies Fear Tells You

Understanding fear's purpose and power

Fear is a master storyteller, spinning lies so convincing they feel like truth. It tells you that you're not strong enough, not smart enough, not ready. It insists that failure is certain and that taking a risk will only lead to pain. Fear's goal isn't to guide you—it's to keep you small, stuck, and "safe."

But here's what fear doesn't want you to know: it's not always right. In fact, fear is often wrong. Its purpose isn't to tell the truth; it's to protect you from the unknown. Fear evolved to keep us alive, to warn us of physical danger like predators or cliffs. The problem is, in modern life, fear doesn't always know the difference between real threats and imagined ones. It reacts to everything as though your survival is at stake.

Fear isn't inherently bad—it's trying to do its job. But its power lies in the stories it convinces you to believe. It says, "Don't speak up; you'll be judged." It says, "Don't try; you'll fail." It says, "Don't step forward; you'll get hurt." These lies keep you from taking risks, chasing dreams, and stepping into the life you truly want.

The truth is, fear is a signal, not a stop sign. It's a flashing light that says, "This matters." And while fear might make you hesitate, it's also proof that you're standing at the edge of something important. Every time fear tries to keep you small, it's really pointing to an opportunity for growth.

You don't have to silence fear completely—just stop letting it make your decisions. Acknowledge it, thank it for trying to protect you, and then move forward anyway. Because when you step through fear, you discover its greatest lie of all: it was never as powerful as you thought.

Fear will tell you lies, but your courage will tell the truth.

Do It Scared

Why waiting for courage means waiting forever

Here's the hard truth: if you're waiting to feel brave before you take the leap, you'll be waiting forever. Courage isn't some magical state of being that appears when the stars align. It's not the absence of fear—it's what you do in the presence of it. The truth is, bravery doesn't come before action; it comes *because* of action.

Fear has a sneaky way of convincing you that you're not ready. It whispers, "Not yet. Maybe tomorrow. Maybe when you're stronger." But the reality is, there will never be a "perfect time" to face your fears. You'll never feel completely ready to take that first step. And that's okay. You don't need to be ready—you just need to move.

Doing it scared means acknowledging your fear and acting anyway. It's making the decision that your goals, your dreams, and your growth are more important than the temporary discomfort of fear. Every step you take, no matter how small, chips away at that fear and builds your confidence. Courage grows through doing—not waiting.

Think about it: the first time you try something new, it's terrifying. But the more you do it, the less scary it becomes. You've proven to yourself that you're capable, that the fear didn't win, and that you're stronger than you thought. That's how courage is built—through messy, imperfect action.

Fear will always be there, waiting to talk you out of what you want. But you don't have to listen. You can move forward, even with your hands shaking and your heart racing. Because the only way to truly conquer fear is to face it head-on.

Do it scared. Do it messy. Do it now. Because waiting for courage only keeps you stuck.

Reclaiming Control

Strategies for facing fear and making it work for you

Fear doesn't have to be the driver in your life. It's time to move it from the front seat to the back, where it belongs. Fear is loud, persistent, and often irrational, but it only has as much power as you give it. Reclaiming control isn't about silencing fear—it's about learning how to manage it and make it work for you.

Here are strategies to face fear and take back your power:

1.   **Name It**

Fear thrives in the unknown. When you feel afraid, take a moment to identify exactly what's scaring you. Is it fear of failure? Fear of judgment? Fear of the unknown? Naming your fear takes away some of its power and allows you to see it for what it is—a reaction, not a reality.

2.   **Separate Fear from Fact**

Fear loves to exaggerate. Challenge the story fear is telling you. Ask yourself, "Is this true? What's the worst that could really happen?" Often, you'll find that fear is blowing things out of proportion. Separating facts from feelings helps you regain perspective.

3.   **Take Small Steps**

You don't have to conquer fear all at once. Start small. Break down what you're afraid of into manageable steps and tackle them one at a time. Every small win builds confidence and chips away at fear's hold on you.

4.   **Use Fear as a Guide**

Fear often points to the things that matter most to you. Instead of running from it, ask yourself, "What is this fear trying to tell me?" Use it as a signal to focus your energy on what's truly important.

5. **Practice Exposure**

The more you face what scares you, the less power it has. Gradually expose yourself to the situations or actions that trigger your fear. With each attempt, you'll grow more comfortable and confident.

6. **Anchor Yourself in the Present**

Fear loves to pull you into the "what-ifs" of the future. Ground yourself in the present moment by focusing on your breath, your surroundings, or something tangible in your environment. This helps you stop spiraling and regain control.

7. **Create a Fear Plan**

If you're worried about a specific situation, create a plan. Think through how you'll handle it step by step. Having a plan reduces uncertainty and makes the fear feel less overwhelming.

Fear will always exist—it's part of being human. But it doesn't have to dictate your life. You have the power to choose how you respond to it. By acknowledging your fear, challenging it, and taking action anyway, you reclaim control and prove to yourself that fear isn't in charge—you are.

Fear might show up, but it doesn't get to drive. Take the wheel and move forward on your terms.

The Freedom in Letting Go

Why clinging to fear keeps you stuck

Fear is a powerful thing. It convinces you that holding on to it will keep you safe, that clinging to its warnings will protect you from pain, failure, or disappointment. But the truth is, holding on to fear only chains you to the very things you're trying to escape. Fear isn't a safety net—it's a cage.

Clinging to fear keeps you stuck in a cycle of avoidance. It stops you from taking risks, speaking your truth, or stepping into opportunities that could change your life. It tells you, "Stay here.

Don't move. It's safer this way." But is it really? Or is it just keeping you from the life you're meant to live?

Letting go of fear doesn't mean you'll never feel it again. It means choosing not to let it control you. It's acknowledging that fear might show up, but it doesn't get to make your decisions. Letting go is about trusting yourself—trusting that you're strong enough to handle whatever comes next, even if it's unknown.

When you let go of fear, you open yourself to freedom. Freedom to try, to fail, to grow, and to succeed. Freedom to live fully, without constantly second-guessing or shrinking away from challenges. Fear will always whisper that letting go is dangerous, but the real danger lies in holding on.

Think about the times fear held you back. What did you miss out on? What could've been different if you'd taken the leap? Now imagine what your life could look like if you stopped letting fear dictate your choices.

The freedom in letting go isn't about banishing fear—it's about choosing courage over comfort. It's about stepping out of fear's shadow and realizing you were never stuck; you were just holding on to the wrong thing.

Let go of fear, and watch how far you can rise.

44 – DERRICK C SOLANO

Prompt

Take a moment to reflect on one fear that's been holding you back. Maybe it's the fear of failure, rejection, or not being enough. Whatever it is, bring it into focus.

1. **Name the Fear:** Write it down. Be specific. What exactly are you afraid of?
2. **Explore Its Impact:** How has this fear affected your decisions, relationships, or goals? What has it cost you—opportunities, peace, growth?
3. **Imagine Freedom:** What would your life look like if this fear no longer held power

over you? How would you act differently? What would you pursue or embrace?

Be honest with yourself. The goal isn't to erase the fear but to recognize the grip it has on you—and to envision the freedom that comes with letting it go.

Because the life you want is on the other side of that fear.

PART THREE: FIRE

"*You are made of fire. Burn brighter, not out.*"

Fire is the force within you that refuses to quit. It's the spark that keeps you moving, the heat that drives your passion, and the light that guides you through the darkness. But like any fire, it needs to be cared for. Left untended, it can burn out—or worse, it can burn you out.

This section is about finding that inner fire, the part of you that refuses to give up no matter what life throws at you. It's about learning how to keep that fire alive, even when the world tries to smother it. Most importantly, it's about rising from the ashes of what tried to destroy you, stronger and more alive than ever before.

Your fire is your power, and it's always within you, waiting to be ignited. Let's explore how to stoke it, protect it, and use it to fuel the life you're meant to live. Because you're not here to flicker—you're here to blaze.

The Ashes Don't Define You

Rising from destruction stronger than before

When life falls apart, it can feel like the end. Whether it's a relationship, a dream, or a version of yourself you thought would last forever, watching it crumble can leave you in ruins. But here's the truth: destruction isn't the end—it's a beginning. The ashes of what's been lost don't define you; they're the foundation for what comes next.

Think about it: fire consumes, but it also purifies. It clears away what no longer serves, leaving behind space for new growth. The same is true for the hardest moments in your life. Losing something, failing, or starting over isn't proof of weakness—it's an opportunity to rebuild, stronger and more aligned with who you're meant to be.

Rising from destruction isn't about ignoring the pain or pretending it didn't happen. It's about acknowledging the loss, learning from it, and choosing to move forward. Every time you rise from the ashes, you prove that you're not defined by what happened to you—you're defined by how you respond to it.

Look at your scars, your failures, and your setbacks. They don't make you less—they make you more. They're reminders that you've been through the fire and come out the other side. Each time you rebuild, you become stronger, more resilient, and more unshakable.

The ashes of your past are not the end of your story. They're the proof that even when everything falls apart, you have the power to rise again—stronger, brighter, and more alive than ever before.

Because the fire didn't destroy you. It made you.

Fanning the Flames

How to keep your inner fire alive during tough times

Life has a way of testing your fire. There will be moments when the world feels heavy, when obstacles pile up, and when the light inside you feels like it's flickering out. But here's the thing: your fire isn't gone—it's just waiting for you to stoke it.

Keeping your inner fire alive during tough times isn't about avoiding struggle; it's about finding ways to fuel your strength, passion, and purpose even in the darkest moments. It's about protecting the flame that keeps you moving forward and nurturing it so it burns brighter.

Here's how to fan the flames when life gets hard:

1. **Protect Your Energy**
    Tough times drain you. Be intentional about setting boundaries with people, tasks, or situations that deplete your fire. You don't have to give everyone access to your energy—save it for what matters most.

2. **Reconnect with Your Why**
    When the fire feels dim, remind yourself why it's burning in the first place. What are you fighting for? What drives you? Revisiting your purpose can reignite your passion and give you the strength to keep going.

3. **Find Small Sparks**
    Even the smallest joys can fuel your fire. Whether it's music, nature, movement, or connecting with someone who lifts you up, these little sparks can remind you of the light within.

4. **Take Care of Your Vessel**

Your body and mind are the home of your fire. Rest when you need it, eat to fuel yourself, and move to keep the energy flowing. Neglecting yourself is like starving the flame—it can't burn if there's no fuel.

5. **Celebrate the Tiny Wins**

Every step forward, no matter how small, is proof that your fire is still burning. Celebrate those wins—they're evidence that you're moving, growing, and thriving.

6. **Trust the Embers**

Even when the fire seems small, trust that the embers are still alive. Sometimes, surviving is enough. Those embers hold the potential to blaze again, stronger than before.

Your fire doesn't have to roar all the time. It can ebb and flow, but it's always there, waiting for you to fan the flames. When life gets tough, don't focus on how bright the fire is—focus on keeping it alive. Because no matter how hard the storm tries to put it out, your fire is yours, and it will always find a way to burn.

Protect it. Nurture it. Let it grow—because your fire is what keeps you alive.

Burn the Bullsh*t

Letting go of perfectionism and societal expectations

Perfectionism is a lie. It's a shiny, polished trap that convinces you to chase something that doesn't exist. Society piles on expectations, telling you to look perfect, act perfect, and never mess up. But here's the truth: perfectionism isn't about being better—it's about control. It keeps you spinning your wheels, exhausted and afraid, trying to live up to standards that were never meant to fit real, messy, human lives.

The only way to truly grow is to burn that bullsh*t down. Let go of the need to be perfect, and stop letting societal expectations define your worth. You weren't put on this earth to fit into a mold someone else designed. You're here to be real, raw, and unapologetically you.

Here's how to start burning the bullsh*t:

1. **Call Out the Lie**
   Recognize where the pressure to be perfect is coming from. Is it social media, your up-bringing, or the fear of judgment? Once you name the source, it becomes easier to reject it.

2. **Redefine Success**
   Stop measuring yourself by someone else's standards. Success doesn't have to mean a six-figure job or flawless appearances. It can mean showing up for yourself, doing what you love, and living a life that feels right for you.

3. **Embrace Your Flaws**
   Perfectionism tells you that flaws are weak-

nesses. That's bullsh*t. Your flaws make you unique, human, and relatable. They're part of your story—own them.

4. **Choose Progress Over Perfection**
Instead of trying to do everything perfectly, focus on moving forward. Progress, no matter how small, is always more valuable than standing still out of fear of messing up.

5. **Stop Apologizing for Existing**
You don't owe anyone an explanation for who you are or how you live your life. Stop apologizing for not being "perfect" and start celebrating the real, messy, beautiful person you are.

When you burn the bullsh*t, you make space for freedom. Freedom to live authentically, to love yourself fully, and to show up without fear of judgment. Letting go of perfectionism isn't easy, but it's the only way to truly feel alive. The world doesn't need another "perfect" person—it needs you, exactly as you are.

Burn the lies. Burn the masks. Burn the bullsh*t—and watch your fire blaze brighter than ever.

The Power of Anger

Turning frustration into action

Anger gets a bad rap. People tell you to "calm down," "let it go," or "be the bigger person." But the truth is, anger isn't the problem—what you do with it is what matters. At its core, anger is energy. It's a signal that something isn't right, that something matters to you deeply. When channeled correctly, anger isn't destructive—it's transformative.

Think of anger as fire. Left uncontrolled, it can burn everything to the ground, including you. But when focused and used intentionally, it can light the path forward. Anger has the power to push you out of complacency, to break you free from fear, and to propel you into action. It's a force, and it's yours to harness.

Here's how to turn your frustration into fuel:

1. **Identify the Source**
    What's making you angry? Is it a situation, a person, or an injustice? Understanding the root of your anger allows you to direct your energy where it can make a difference instead of letting it spiral.

2. **Reframe It as Motivation**
    Instead of seeing anger as something to suppress, use it as a motivator. Let it remind you of what you care about and what you're willing to fight for. Anger isn't just frustration—it's passion waiting to be redirected.

3. **Take Productive Action**
    Use your anger to fuel tangible steps forward. Whether it's speaking up, making a change, or tackling a problem head-on, ac-

tion transforms anger from a weight into momentum.

4.   **Set Boundaries**
Sometimes, anger arises from letting people or situations overstep your limits. Use it as a reminder to protect your peace and prioritize yourself. Setting boundaries isn't selfish—it's survival.

5.   **Create Something from It**
Anger can be a powerful creative force. Write it, paint it, move your body through it. Channeling your frustration into creation not only releases the tension but turns it into something meaningful.

Anger isn't a weakness, and it's not something to fear. It's a natural response to pain, injustice, or unmet needs. But it doesn't have to consume you. When you learn to control it, focus it, and use it, anger becomes one of the most powerful tools you have for change.

So don't just feel angry—use it. Let it push you, ignite you, and remind you that you're alive.

Prompt

Take a moment to reflect on the parts of your life that are holding you back—the things that weigh you down, drain your energy, or keep you stuck.

1. **Identify the Bullsh*t:** What habits, relationships, fears, or beliefs are no longer serving you? What feels heavy or toxic? Write them down.
2. **Ask Why You're Holding On:** What are you afraid of losing if you let these things go? Is the fear keeping you in a cycle you don't want to be in?

3. **Visualize the Burn:** Imagine setting fire to the things that don't belong in your life anymore. What would your life look like without them? How would it feel to be free of them?

Be honest with yourself. This isn't about small changes—it's about the kind of transformation that comes from burning down what no longer serves you so you can rise stronger from the ashes.

Because sometimes, to find your fire, you have to let the rest burn.

PART FOUR: RESILIENCE

"*You've survived every storm so far. Keep going.*"

Resilience isn't about never falling—it's about getting back up every time life knocks you down. It's the strength you build when you face the storms of life and refuse to let them break you. It's not flashy or perfect; it's raw, gritty, and deeply personal. Resilience is what keeps you moving forward, even when the world feels like it's crumbling around you.

This section is about learning how to weather the storms and build a foundation so strong that no matter what life throws at you, you'll remain standing. It's about recognizing the strength you already have and finding ways to fortify it even more.

You've been through hell before, and you've made it out. Every setback, every heartbreak, every failure has prepared you for the challenges ahead. Resilience isn't something you're born with—it's something you create, piece by piece, through every trial you face.

Let's focus on what it means to be unshakable, to turn your pain into power, and to keep moving forward, no matter what. Because the storms will come, but you've already proven you have what it takes to survive them.

What Resilience Really Is

The truth about staying strong when life gets hard

Resilience is often misunderstood. People think it means being tough all the time, never breaking, or always having it together. But that's not resilience—that's a myth. Real resilience isn't about being unbreakable; it's about what you do after you've been broken. It's about showing up for yourself, even when everything feels heavy and impossible.

Resilience is messy. It's the willingness to keep going, even when you're scared, tired, or unsure. It's falling down and getting back up, over and over again. It's not about avoiding pain or pretending it doesn't exist—it's about finding the strength to face it and move through it.

Staying strong doesn't mean you never feel weak. It means that, despite the weakness, you keep showing up. It's crying in the dark and standing tall in the light. It's allowing yourself to feel everything—the fear, the anger, the sadness—and still deciding not to give up.

Here's the truth: life will test you. It will throw storms your way, and sometimes, it will knock you flat on your back. But resilience is knowing that the storm will pass and that you'll stand again. It's trusting yourself enough to keep going, even when you don't know what's next.

Resilience doesn't mean you have all the answers. It means you're willing to find them. It doesn't mean you're fearless—it means you act in spite of fear. Resilience is built through every challenge, every scar, and every small victory. It's not about being perfect; it's about being persistent.

Resilience isn't a destination—it's a decision. And every time you choose to keep going, you're proving just how strong you really are.

78 – DERRICK C SOLANO

Layering Strength

Using every failure and setback as a foundation for growth

Every failure, every setback, every moment when life knocked you down has something to teach you. At first, it may feel like these experiences are breaking you, but in reality, they're building you. Each challenge you face adds a new layer to your resilience—a layer of strength that makes you stronger than you were before.

Think of life as a series of layers. Every time you fail, every time something doesn't go as planned, you have a choice: let it define you, or let it refine you. When you choose the latter, you're not ignoring the pain—you're using it. Each failure becomes a stepping stone, a piece of your foundation that makes you more unshakable.

Here's how layering strength works:

1.   **Acknowledge the Setback**
     Pretending it didn't happen doesn't help. Face the failure, feel the disappointment, and then decide to move forward.

2.   **Find the Lesson**
     Every setback has something to teach you. What went wrong? What can you do differently next time? Growth comes from understanding, not avoidance.

3.   **Build on What You've Learned**
     Use the lessons from your past to guide your future. Let each failure add to your knowledge and your resilience. With every mistake, you're becoming more equipped to handle whatever comes next.

4.   **Keep Moving Forward**
     Resilience is about persistence. Setbacks

may slow you down, but they don't have to stop you. Every time you choose to keep going, you're adding another layer of strength.

5.   **Embrace the Process**
Growth isn't linear. It's messy, unpredictable, and often uncomfortable. But with each experience—good or bad—you're adding to the foundation of who you are.

Layering strength means recognizing that failure isn't the opposite of success—it's part of it. Each setback is another opportunity to learn, grow, and rebuild stronger. Over time, these layers of resilience form a foundation that's unshakable.

You are the sum of every challenge you've overcome, every lesson you've learned, and every time you've refused to give up. Let your strength build, one layer at a time.

The Unseen Work

The importance of showing up for yourself every day

Resilience isn't built in a single moment. It's not the grand gestures or the big victories that make you strong—it's the quiet, unseen work you do every day. It's the moments when nobody is watching, and you still choose to show up for yourself. That's where the real strength grows.

The unseen work is in the decisions you make when it would be easier to give up. It's getting out of bed when the weight of the world feels crushing. It's saying "yes" to yourself when self-doubt is screaming "no." It's doing the small, consistent things that remind you who you are and what you're capable of.

Here's why the unseen work matters:

1. **It Builds Habits of Strength**
    Every time you show up, even in the smallest way, you're reinforcing the habit of re-silience. It might feel insignificant now, but over time, those small efforts add up to something unshakable.

2. **It's Proof of Your Commitment**
    Showing up for yourself is an act of self-re-spect. It's a declaration that you're worth the effort, no matter how hard it feels.

3. **It Creates Momentum**
    Even the smallest action can spark forward motion. One step turns into two, and before you know it, you're moving through chal-lenges you once thought were impossible.

4. **It's Your Foundation in the Storm**
    Life is unpredictable, and there will be times when everything feels like it's falling apart.

The unseen work is what anchors you in those moments. It's the strength you've built when things were calm, ready to support you when the storms hit.

5.   **It's a Daily Act of Rebellion Against Giving Up**

Choosing to show up is defiance against every reason not to. It's your way of saying, "I'm still here. I'm still trying. I'm not done."

Resilience isn't about perfection. It's about persistence. Some days, the unseen work will feel small—a single step forward. Other days, it will feel monumental, like climbing a mountain. But what matters is that you keep showing up, day after day, building strength one decision at a time.

Because when you show up for yourself, you prove that you're worth fighting for—even when no one else is watching.

CHAPTER

Living Unbreakably

How to stay grounded and strong no matter what life throws at you

Living unbreakably doesn't mean life stops throwing punches—it means you learn to take the hits and keep moving. It's about staying grounded in who you are, even when the world around you feels chaotic or uncertain. It's about trusting your own strength and refusing to let life's challenges define you.

Here's the truth: being unbreakable doesn't mean you'll never bend or feel pain. It means that no matter what happens, you'll find a way to rise. It's a mindset, a choice, and a way of showing up for yourself every day. Living unbreakably is about building a foundation so strong that nothing—no storm, no setback, no failure—can destroy it.

Here's how to live unbreakably:

1. **Anchor Yourself in Your Values**
   Know what matters most to you. When life gets chaotic, having clear values—whether it's integrity, love, or resilience—keeps you grounded and gives you a compass to navigate through the storm.

2. **Strengthen Your Inner Voice**
   The world will try to tell you who to be and how to live. Tune out the noise and listen to your own voice. Remind yourself of your worth, your strength, and your ability to handle whatever comes your way.

3. **Focus on What You Can Control**
   Life throws curveballs, and you can't control everything. But you can control how you respond. Focus your energy on what you can

change—your actions, your mindset, and your choices.

4.   **Lean on Your Resilience Toolkit**
Over time, you've built tools for survival—habits, lessons, and coping strategies. Use them. When life gets tough, go back to what has worked for you in the past and trust in your ability to adapt.

5.   **Stay Present in the Moment**
Worrying about the future or replaying the past only adds to the weight you carry. Stay present. Focus on what's in front of you and take it one step at a time.

6.   **Celebrate Your Strength**
You've survived everything life has thrown at you so far. That's not luck—it's strength. Recognize and celebrate the resilience you've built, and let it fuel you for the road ahead.

7.   **Choose to Keep Rising**
Living unbreakably isn't about avoiding challenges; it's about choosing to rise every single time. It's a decision to keep fighting

for the life you want, no matter what stands in your way.

You are unbreakable not because life is easy, but because you've made it through the hardest moments and come out stronger. Every time you face a challenge, every time you choose to keep going, you prove to yourself—and the world—that nothing can destroy the fire inside you.

Living unbreakably is about showing up, standing strong, and believing in your resilience no matter what life throws your way. You've done it before, and you'll do it again.

Prompt

Take a moment to reflect on your journey and identify three times in your life when you thought the pain, fear, or uncertainty was too much to bear—moments when you didn't think you'd make it through.

1. **Write Them Down:** Be specific about what happened. What made these moments feel impossible?

2. **Acknowledge Your Strength:** How did you get through each of these experiences? What inner strength or external support helped you survive?

3. **Recognize Your Resilience:** Reflect on how these moments shaped you. What did you learn? How did they contribute to the person you are today?

You've already proven to yourself that you can survive the impossible. Let these moments serve as a reminder that no matter what challenges come your way, you have the strength to rise again.

Because if you made it through those moments, you can make it through anything.

PART FIVE: FREEDOM

"Freedom starts when you stop asking for permission to exist."

Freedom isn't about having no limits or responsibilities—it's about living on your terms. It's about shedding the expectations, judgments, and pressures that have kept you small and stepping fully into who you are. Real freedom comes from within, from the moment you decide you're done living for others and ready to live for yourself.

This section is about reclaiming your power and choosing authenticity over approval. It's about embracing every piece of yourself—the messy, the imperfect, and the beautiful—and showing up unapologetically as you are. True freedom isn't something you wait for; it's something you create by letting go of fear, shame, and the need for validation.

Let's explore what it means to live authentically, boldly, and without apology. Because the life you've been waiting for isn't somewhere out there—it's inside you, waiting to be claimed.

Owning Your Truth

How to stop hiding behind masks

We all wear masks. Maybe it's the mask of perfection to hide our flaws, the mask of strength to cover up our pain, or the mask of indifference to protect ourselves from rejection. But the longer we wear them, the more we lose sight of who we really are. Owning your truth means letting go of those masks and choosing to live authentically, even when it feels vulnerable.

Hiding behind a mask might feel safe, but it's exhausting. It creates distance between you and the people around you, and more importantly, it creates distance between you and yourself. You can't truly connect with others—or live freely—if you're constantly pretending to be someone you're not.

Here's how to start owning your truth:

1. **Identify the Masks You Wear**
   Ask yourself: What parts of me am I hiding? Who am I trying to impress or protect? Recognizing the masks is the first step to letting them go.

2. **Acknowledge the Fear Behind Them**
   Masks are often born out of fear—fear of judgment, rejection, or failure. What are you afraid will happen if you show the real you? Naming those fears helps you see them for what they are—barriers, not truths.

3. **Start Small**
   Owning your truth doesn't mean you have to bare your soul all at once. Start by being honest with yourself about your feelings, needs, and desires. Then, practice sharing

small pieces of your truth with people you trust.

4. **Embrace Your Imperfections**
The person you truly are—the one beneath the mask—isn't perfect. And that's okay. Authenticity comes from accepting your flaws, not hiding them. Your imperfections are what make you real and relatable.

5. **Surround Yourself with Acceptance**
Spend time with people who value the real you, not the version you think they want. The right people will respect and love you for your authenticity.

Owning your truth is a process. It takes courage to step out from behind the masks you've worn for so long. But every time you do, you reclaim a piece of yourself. You create deeper connections with the world around you, and you remind yourself that who you are is already enough.

Because freedom starts with honesty, and owning your truth is the first step to living unapologetically.

Rewriting Your Narrative

Letting go of the stories others wrote for you

From the moment we're born, other people start writing our story. Family, society, and culture all weigh in on who we're supposed to be, how we're supposed to act, and what we're allowed to want. These narratives can shape our lives, often without us realizing it. But here's the truth: the story others wrote for you isn't the one you have to live.

Rewriting your narrative means letting go of the expectations, labels, and limitations imposed on you by others. It's about deciding who you are for yourself—on your terms—and reclaiming the pen to write a story that feels true to you.

Here's how to begin:

1. **Identify the Old Story**
    What are the beliefs or expectations you've been living by? Maybe it's "I have to be perfect to be loved" or "Success means sacrificing my happiness." Write down the narratives you've been carrying that no longer serve you.

2. **Challenge the Lies**
    Ask yourself: Who gave me this story? Is it even true? Often, these narratives are based on fear, control, or someone else's unresolved issues. Recognizing this helps you break free from their grip.

3. **Define Your Truth**
    What do you want your story to be? Who are you when you strip away everyone else's

expectations? Take the time to define your values, goals, and desires—this is the foundation of your new narrative.

4.   **Take Action to Live Your Story**

A rewritten narrative only comes to life when you start living it. That means making choices that align with your truth, even when they feel uncomfortable or scary. Each action reinforces the new story you're creating.

5.   **Release the Need for Approval**

Letting go of the old story might upset people who benefited from the version of you that fit their expectations. That's okay. Your story is yours, and you don't need anyone's permission to live it.

Rewriting your narrative isn't about erasing the past—it's about learning from it and choosing to move forward differently. It's about recognizing that you are not the product of someone else's imagination, but the author of your own life.

You have the power to write a story that reflects who you truly are. Take the pen, and start creating the life you deserve.

Loving Yourself Loudly

The power of self-acceptance and self-love

Loving yourself isn't selfish—it's necessary. But in a world that constantly tells you to change, to be quieter, smaller, or more "acceptable," self-love can feel like rebellion. And that's exactly what it is: a bold, unapologetic declaration that you are enough, just as you are.

Loving yourself loudly means no longer hiding behind shame, doubt, or fear. It's about embracing every part of who you are—your flaws, your strengths, your scars—and showing up fully for yourself. It's not quiet or hesitant. It's fierce, un-apologetic, and transformative.

Here's why self-love matters and how to live it loudly:

1. **Self-Acceptance is the Foundation**
    True self-love begins with acceptance. It's recognizing that you don't need to be per-fect to be worthy. The moment you stop fighting who you are and start embracing it, you create space for growth, peace, and free-dom.

2. **You Set the Standard**
    The way you treat yourself teaches others how to treat you. Loving yourself loudly sets the tone for the respect, kindness, and love you allow into your life. If you don't show up for yourself, why should anyone else?

3. **Love Your Whole Self**
    Self-love isn't just about celebrating your strengths; it's about holding space for your imperfections too. It's loving the messy, bro-ken, and vulnerable parts of yourself that

you've been told to hide. These are the pieces that make you real.

4. **Celebrate Your Wins**

Stop brushing off your accomplishments or waiting for someone else to validate you. Celebrate every step forward, every hard-earned victory, and every moment you choose yourself. You've worked for it—own it.

5. **Speak Your Love Out Loud**

Replace the inner critic with an inner cheerleader. Speak to yourself the way you'd speak to someone you love. Out loud, in writing, or in your mind, remind yourself daily: "I am enough. I am worthy. I am loved."

6. **Refuse to Dim Your Light**

Stop shrinking to fit into spaces that weren't meant for you. Loving yourself loudly means standing tall in your truth, even when it makes others uncomfortable. Your light isn't too bright—it's exactly as it should be.

When you choose to love yourself loudly, you're not just transforming your relationship with yourself—you're giving others permission to do the same. You become a force of authenticity and confidence, unshaken by the noise of outside expectations.

Love yourself unapologetically, fiercely, and out loud—because you are worth it, every single day.

The Joy of Imperfection

Finding peace in the messy, beautiful chaos of life

Life is messy. It's full of mistakes, detours, and moments where things don't go as planned. And that's okay. The truth is, perfection is an illusion—a shiny goalpost that keeps moving further away the closer you get to it. Chasing it only leaves you exhausted and disappointed. Real joy comes from letting go of the need to be perfect and finding beauty in the chaos instead.

Imperfection is where life truly happens. It's in the flaws, the unexpected turns, and the moments that don't go according to plan that we grow, learn, and discover who we really are. When you stop trying to control every detail and start embracing the mess, you open yourself up to peace, connection, and a deeper sense of self.

Here's how to find joy in imperfection:

1. **Let Go of the Script**
   Stop holding yourself to impossible standards. Life doesn't follow a script, and neither should you. Give yourself permission to adapt, change course, and figure it out as you go.

2. **Celebrate the Flaws**
   The cracks and imperfections in your life aren't weaknesses—they're part of your story. Embrace them. They make you unique and real, and they're often where the most beautiful moments begin.

3. **Be Present**
   Perfectionism pulls you into the future, al-

ways worrying about what's next or what could go wrong. Imperfection grounds you in the present, where life is actually happening. Focus on what's in front of you and find joy in the here and now.

4. **Practice Self-Compassion**

Perfection demands that you beat yourself up for every mistake. Joy in imperfection means forgiving yourself and learning from those moments instead. You're human—embrace it.

5. **Find Beauty in the Chaos**

Some of life's most meaningful moments come from unexpected places. The mess, the struggle, the in-between—it's all part of the masterpiece. Look for the beauty in the imperfect and let it remind you that life doesn't have to be perfect to be amazing.

Imperfection isn't a flaw to fix—it's a truth to embrace. When you stop chasing an unattainable version of life and start leaning into its natural chaos, you discover freedom. You stop living for some future ideal and start experiencing the messy, beautiful joy that's already here.

Because life isn't perfect, and it doesn't have to be. The beauty is in the imperfections—and so are you.

Prompt

Take a moment to imagine your life without the constant pressure to meet everyone else's expectations.

1. **Reflect on Your Current Reality:** How much of your energy is spent trying to make others happy or gain their approval? What are you sacrificing—your time, dreams, or authenticity?

2. **Visualize the Shift:** What would change if you stopped prioritizing other people's opinions? Would you pursue different goals, make bolder choices, or feel freer?

3. **Write It Down:** Describe the version of your life where you live unapologetically for yourself. What does it look like? How does it feel?

Let this reflection be a reminder that you don't need permission to live your truth.

Because the life you've been waiting for starts the moment you stop trying to please others.

Final Affirmation

"This is not the end of your story. It's the beginning of your strength."

No matter where you are right now—whether you're rebuilding, struggling, or thriving—this moment is not the finish line. It's a turning point. Every challenge you've faced, every scar you carry, and every fear you've overcome has prepared you for this.

Your story is still being written, and the next chapter is yours to create. This is the moment you choose strength, resilience, and freedom. This is where you rise, step into your truth, and live unapologetically as the powerful, unbreakable force you are.

Your strength begins now. Keep going—you've got this.

Acknowledgments

To the readers who picked up this book and decided to take a chance—not just on these words, but on yourselves—thank you. This journey of self-discovery, resilience, and unapologetic truth wouldn't exist without your courage. By opening these pages, you've already taken the first step toward owning your strength and rewriting your story.

Thank you for trusting this book to be part of your journey. Your willingness to face the messy, imperfect, and powerful parts of who you are is what inspires everything I write. Together, we prove that resilience isn't just possible—it's inevitable for those who refuse to stay down.

You are the reason these words exist. Keep going. You're stronger than you know.

Derrick Solano is a raw, unfiltered storyteller and author of *I Won't Break*, *Vexture*, *NAKED*, and *Fck Perfect**. His work dives deep into themes of resilience, authenticity, and embracing imperfection, offering readers practical tools and unapologetic truths to navigate life's toughest moments. Derrick's journey—from surviving trauma and battling addiction to finding strength in scars—has shaped his unique voice, one that resonates with anyone fighting to rebuild their life. Through his books, music, and raw insights, Derrick empowers readers to rise, fight, and live unbreakably.